Author:

David Stewart has written many nonfiction books for children. He lives in Brighton, England, with his family.

Artist:

Amerigo Pinelli is a freelance illustrator based in Naples, Italy. He studied illustration at Štěpán Zavřel Foundation's International School of Illustration and has worked in animation and publishing.

Series creator:

David Salariya was born in Dundee, Scotland. He has illustrated a wide range of books and has created and designed many new series for publishers in the UK and overseas. David established The Salariya Book Company in 1989. He lives in Brighton with his wife, illustrator Shirley Willis, and their son, Jonathan.

Editor: **Nick Pierce**

Photo credits:

p.22–23 FloridaStock/Shutterstock, Keith Levit/Shutterstock, Igor Batenev/Shutterstock
p.24–25 Nagel Photography/Shutterstock, Michele Aldeghi/Shutterstock, emperorcosar/Shutterstock, OSTILL is Franck Camhi/Shutterstock, thka/Shutterstock, Vladimir Wrangel/Shutterstock, Kichigin/Shutterstock

Published in Great Britain in 2021 by
The Salariya Book Company Ltd
25 Marlborough Place, Brighton BN1 1UB

ISBN 978-0-531-13177-0 (lib. bdg.) 978-0-531-13190-9 (pbk.)

All rights reserved.
Published in 2021 in the United States
by Franklin Watts®
An imprint of Scholastic Inc.

A CIP catalog record for this book is available from the Library of Congress.

Printed in the U.S.A. 113
1 2 3 4 5 6 7 8 9 10 R 28 27 26 25 24 23 22 21

SCHOLASTIC, FRANKLIN WATTS, and associated logo are trademarks and/or registered trademarks of Scholastic In

Scholastic Inc., 557 Broadway, New York, NY 10012

How Would You Survive as a Polar Bear?

Written by
David Stewart

Illustrated by
Amerigo Pinelli

Series created by
David Salariya

Franklin Watts®
An Imprint of Scholastic Inc.

Contents

You Are a Polar Bear

Another name for the polar bear is "ice bear." It's an appropriate name for you, since wild polar bears spend their lives in the frozen landscape of the Arctic. It's a very difficult life: You have to hunt for your prey across the sea ice, and your hunting grounds are shrinking every year. You're the largest land predator in the world, so you need to find a lot of prey to survive. As a female polar bear, you also have the responsibility of raising your cubs and making sure that they can fend for themselves once they're old enough. It's time to answer the big question: How would you survive as a polar bear?

A Polar Bear's Body

Fur

Your fur is very oily and repels water, helping you to swim better.

Nose

Your nose is one of the few areas of your body not covered in fur. You have a very keen sense of smell, which you use to track your prey.

Weight

Male polar bears weigh around 1,500 pounds (680.4 kilograms), while female polar bears (like you) weigh about half as much.

Front paws

You have small depressions on your front paws that provide a grip when you're walking on slippery ice.

Height

On average, all polar bears are 3.5 to 5 feet (1 to 1.5 meters) tall when standing on all four legs. On your hind legs, you reach a height of 7 feet (2.1 meters), while male polar bears can reach 10 feet (3 meters) in height.

Skin

Underneath your fur, your skin is black. This helps you absorb the heat of the Sun to stay warm in the cold climate.

Claws

Your claws are roughly 2 to 3 inches (5 to 7 centimeters) long. Ideal for tearing into prey!

Paws

Your paws are much bigger than those of other bear species—about 12 inches (30.5 centimeters) across. They work like snowshoes, spreading your weight across a wider surface area so that you don't sink into the snow as you walk across it.

The Arctic Circle

Y our home, the Arctic Circle, is a very cold and inhospitable place to live. Polar bears roam the Arctic regions of the United States (Alaska), Canada, Russia, Norway, and Greenland. At the North Pole, the temperature can drop as low as -70°F (-56.7°C). Fortunately, you have a 4-inch-thick (10.2-centimeter) layer of fat underneath your skin that stops the cold from penetrating your body and killing you.

If You...

need to hide, your white fur is the perfect camouflage for blending in with the snowy Arctic environment.

Other Animals of the Arctic:

Despite the difficult conditions, there are many other species of animal that live in the Arctic:

Arctic wolf

Reindeer

Puffin

Seal

Walrus

Arctic fox

Narwhal

As a predator, you're completely dependent on the sea ice that forms in the Arctic zone, since your prey lives in the water underneath: You hunt seals, walruses, and narwhals. It's partly for this reason that you're often classified as a "marine mammal."

9

How a Polar Bear Hunts

You can move quickly, on land and in the water. You can reach a top speed of 25 miles per hour (40.2 kilometers per hour) running on land, and swim at a speed of 6 miles per hour (9.7 kilometers per hour). That sounds fast, right? Sadly, your prey, like seals, narwhals, and walruses, can swim much faster. So you need to be more clever than your prey in order to not go hungry. As a polar bear, you have lots of crafty hunting techniques for outsmarting dinner...

Still hunting (below): Stalking (right):

This is the polar bear's most common hunting method.
1. You use your sense of smell to find a seal's breathing hole in the thick ice.
2. You crouch silently nearby, waiting patiently, sometimes for hours, for a seal to appear.
3. When it does, you quickly reach in with a forepaw and drag it out onto the ice.
4. Then you bite its head to crush its skull. Now you can eat!

You can also stalk a seal across the ice.
1. You see a seal, and then crouch down about 100 yards (90 meters) away from it. If it doesn't notice you, then you slowly start creeping closer.
2. Once you're about 30 to 40 feet (9 to 12 meters) from the unsuspecting seal, you rush forward and attack it.

If You...

are struggling to find food in the months of late summer and early fall, you will have to fast like other polar bears. During this time, polar bears cannot hunt for seals because the sea is unfrozen.

1

2

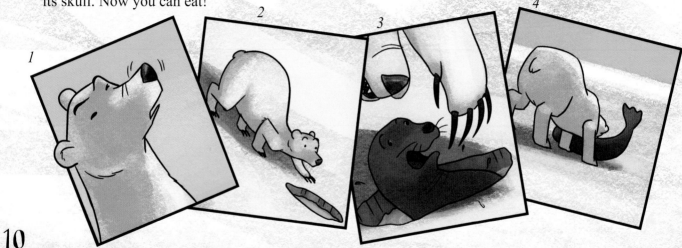

Most of the time, you will fail to catch the seal you're hunting. But if you use your clever techniques and hunt for many months on the ice, you should catch enough prey to not go hungry.

11

Fighting for a Partner

Female polar bears can breed from when they are around four years old. Since they have to face fierce competition to mate, males do not typically get to breed until they're around eight. Male polar bears will follow a female polar bear's tracks for more than 60 miles (96.5 kilometers) for the chance to mate. As a female, you will lead a male bear across the ice and over mountains as part of the mating process. Scientists think that this might be a way for you to test that the male bear is fit and healthy enough to be a father.

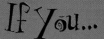

If You...

are approaching your 25th birthday, you probably can't expect to live much longer. Twenty-five is the average life expectancy for a polar bear.

◀ Polar bears are polygynous. This means that the male mates and lives with multiple females, but the females only mate with the one male.

◀ Male polar bears fight over females by standing on their hind legs and growling at each other. Then they swipe at each other with their paws, trying to knock each other down.

▶ Males can end up seriously injured after a fight. They may be left scarred, or lose teeth and fur.

During a fight over a female polar bear, the two males will try to bite each other's face and legs. It can be very vicious.

Getting Ready to Give Birth

Once your mate has left and you're pregnant, you'll need to make a maternity den. This is an ice cave that female polar bears carve out with their claws. First, you need to tunnel a hole into an ice bank, then you pack snow inside it to make a room. Then you climb inside and wait for a fresh snowfall to cover up the entrance. The den provides a safe, warm place for you to rest during your pregnancy and give birth to your cubs.

If You...

are in a deep resting state, your body temperature will not decrease as it would for most other species of mammal in the same circumstances.

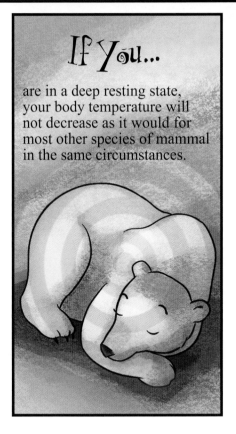

During pregnancy and before entering your den, you eat massive amounts of food, often more than doubling your body weight.

In your den, you enter a deep resting phase, where you breathe more slowly and your heart rate slows from 42 to 27 beats per minute. Polar bears do not hibernate.

Male polar bears don't enter this resting state. They have a genetic adaptation that allows their bodies to produce enough heat to survive the winter months in the Arctic environment.

Mothers and Cubs

Your cubs will be born between the months of November and February. Polar bear cubs are born blind, with a light downy fur, and weighing only 1 pound (0.45 kilograms). Typically, a female polar bear will have a litter of two cubs. You will stay in the den with your cubs until mid-February, or as late as mid-April, nursing them on your milk. You haven't eaten the whole time you've been in the den and are starving. Once your cubs are strong enough, it'll be time to leave the den.

If You...

are nursing your cubs, you will do it in a sitting position, or lying down on your side or your back.

▼ Up to 35 percent of a female polar bear's milk is fat. This makes it highly nutritious for your cubs, helping them grow quickly.

▲ For about 12 to 15 days, your family spends time outside the den while still remaining near it.

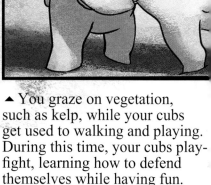

▲ You graze on vegetation, such as kelp, while your cubs get used to walking and playing. During this time, your cubs play-fight, learning how to defend themselves while having fun.

16

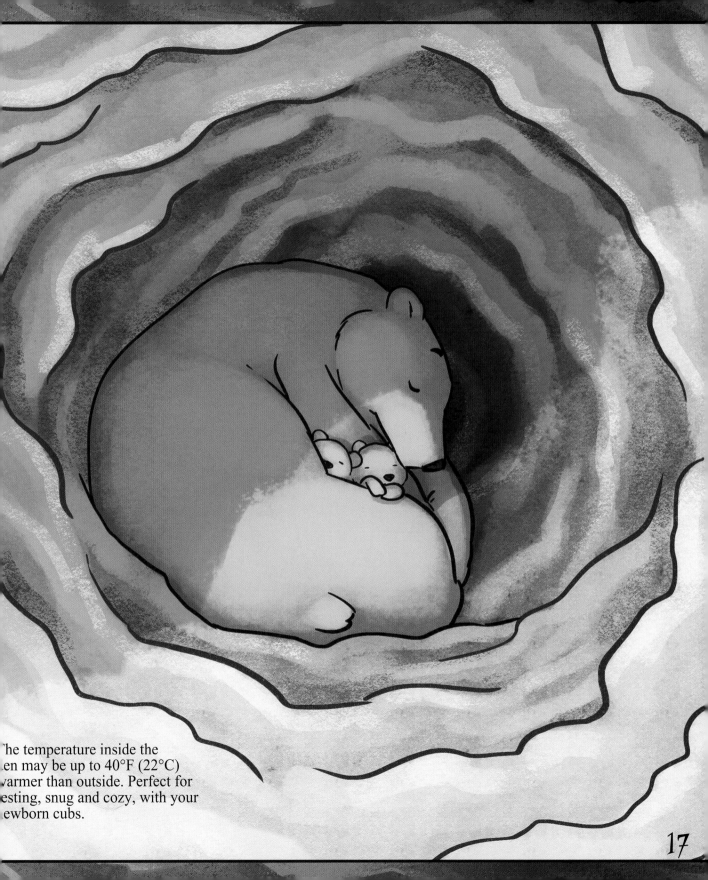

The temperature inside the
den may be up to 40°F (22°C)
warmer than outside. Perfect for
resting, snug and cozy, with your
newborn cubs.

Teaching Your Cubs

Once your cubs are old and strong enough, you'll begin the long trek from your den to the sea ice, where you can hunt for seals. More than half of all cubs die before they're a year old, so you'll have to work hard to keep yours alive by protecting them from dangers and finding them enough food to survive. You use your large, warm body to shelter their smaller ones from the icy winds that blow across the Arctic region as you make your way to the sea ice.

If You...

encounter areas of deep snow or deep water, you might carry your cubs on your back for a while.

◄ During this time, your cubs watch and mimic your hunting methods to prepare for adult life, when they will need to hunt for themselves.

▼ Female polar bears show great courage in defending their cubs. If another polar bear tries to attack them, you will put your cubs behind you and fight to the death to save their lives.

▼ After about two years, once your cubs are strong enough to survive on their own, you will abandon them or chase them away.

Traditionally, Indigenous Peoples would use dogs to chase polar bears down and corner them, and then kill the bears with arrows and spears. Today, dogs are still used, but the arrows and spears have been replaced with guns.

What Are the Dangers?

Quick, run! You might be the biggest predator in the Arctic, but even you can be hunted. Indigenous Peoples who live in Arctic regions have hunted polar bears for thousands of years—not for sport, but for sustenance. Although these hunters kill individual bears, they have never endangered the survival of the species. However, when people from elsewhere started coming in and hunting polar bears, too—for sport, not survival—the numbers being killed increased dramatically.

are an adult polar bear you have no predators to worry about—except for other polar bears, who sometimes commit cannibalism.

Indigenous hunters use nearly every part of a polar bear they've killed. They eat the meat, use the fat as fuel, use the hide to make pants and boots, dry out the gallbladder and heart for medicine, and keep the teeth as talismans.

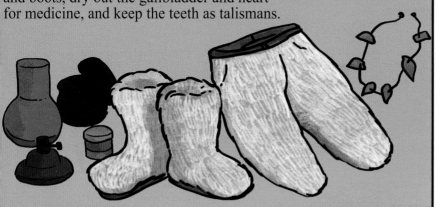

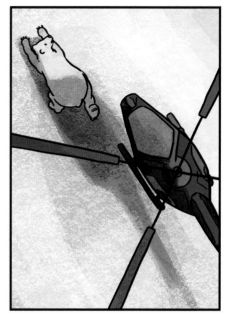

▶ Nonindigenous hunters have used helicopters and snowmobiles to chase down polar bears so that they can shoot them with rifles from a safe distance.

Polar Bears and Climate Change

The life of a polar bear has become much harder in recent decades, as a result of climate change. Scientists are studying the changing behavior of polar bears as they adapt to survive in a new and harsher world.

1. *The sea ice in the Arctic is shrinking because of warming sea temperatures caused by climate change. Without ice to hunt on, polar bears are unable to catch seals, putting them in danger of starving.*

2. Polar bears who can't catch as many seals try to find other prey instead. They hunt whales, walruses, caribou, fish, and ducks to supplement their diet. They've even been observed eating garbage left by humans that they find in towns near their homes.

3. Scientists study polar bears to see how they're adapting or failing to adapt to climate change. Sometimes they sedate polar bears to see what is in their stomachs, or if they're going hungry.

4. Scientists also put transmitters on polar bears so that they can monitor them by satellite and keep count of their numbers.

5. Unless the effects of climate change are reduced, polar bears may lose their hunting grounds entirely and become extinct in the wild.

Polar Bear Family Tree

Polar bears are part of the Caniformia group of mammal species. These species are typically carnivorous and have long snouts and claws. This family tree shows some of the different related species of bear and other closely related mammals in the Caniformia group. If you were a polar bear, these would be some of your closest cousins...

Brown Bear

These large bears are omnivores, meaning they will eat both meat and plants. Some have black or cream-colored hair instead of brown.

Polar Bear (You)

This species, along with the brown bear, is the largest land carnivore in existence, although its reliance on sea ice to hunt means that it is often categorized as a marine mammal!

American Black Bear

This is the world's most common bear species. They eat either meat or plants, depending on their location and the time of year. They are recognizable by their black hair and distinctive, tall ears.

Asian Black Bear

These medium-sized bears have a very distinctive white patch on their chest, sometimes in a "v" shape. They can be very aggressive toward humans.

Dog

Species like dogs, wolves, coyotes, and jackals are all medium-sized Caniformia mammals. They all have a very good sense of smell.

Giant Panda

These adorable black and white bears, native to south central China, spend most of their time munching on bamboo.

Seal

They might be polar bears' prey, but the two species are also related! Seals are large Caniformia mammals that use their flippers to swim quickly through the water.

Polar Bear Quiz

1 What kind of mammal are polar bears often classified as?

2 What do polar bears have on their front paws?

3 What color is polar bears' skin?

4 What is the average life expectancy for a polar bear?

5 What do female polar bears build when they're pregnant?

6 Roughly how long do a mother polar bear and her cubs stay outside their den before making the trek to the sea ice?

7 How many cubs survive beyond their first year of life?

8 What animal do Indigenous Peoples sometimes use to hunt polar bears?

9 What part of a polar bear do Indigenous Peoples sometimes keep as a talisman?

10 How far will a male polar bear follow a female's tracks?

Polar Bear Quiz Answers

1 Marine
(page 9)

2 Small depressions that help them grip
(page 6)

3 Black
(page 7)

4 25 years
(page 12)

5 A maternity den
(page 15)

6 12 to 15 days
(page 16)

7 Less than half
(page 19)

8 Dogs
(page 20)

9 Teeth
(page 21)

10 More than 60 miles (96.5 kilometers)
(page 12)

Polar Bear Facts

There are only around 22,000–31,000 polar bears still in existence.

Sixty to eighty percent of polar bears live in Canada.

A polar bear was the mascot for the 1988 Winter Olympics held in Calgary, Canada.

It is predicted that global polar bear numbers will have declined by 30 percent by 2050.

Because of their low numbers and shrinking habitat, polar bears have been officially classified as a vulnerable species by the IUCN (International Union for Conservation of Nature) Polar Bear Specialist Group in 2015.

A polar bear will ask another polar bear permission for something, such as sharing the carcass of an animal it has killed to eat, by touching noses with the other bear.

Where Do Bears Live?

There are only eight surviving species of bear, and they are found on the continents of Europe, Asia, and North and South America. The map below describes where polar bears and other species of bear live in the wild.

Polar bears live in the Arctic regions of Denmark (Greenland), Norway, Russia, Canada, and the United States.

Brown bears are found in northern Europe, Russia, China, central Asia, the United States, and Canada.

The Asian black bear lives in the forests of Eastern Asia, from Afghanistan to Taiwan and Japan.

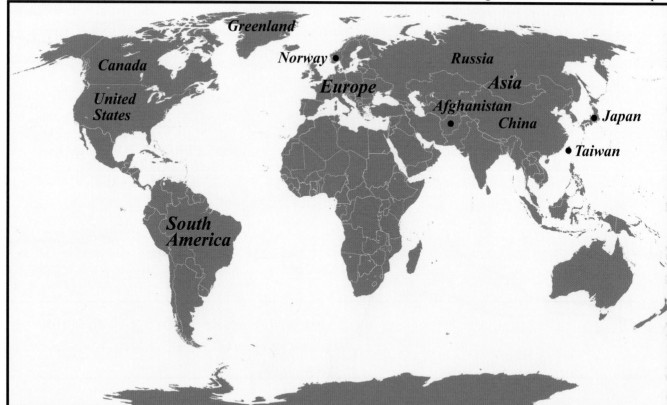

The American black bear, as its name would suggest, is native to North America.

The small spectacled bear is found in the Andean jungles of South America.

The Giant Panda is native to south central China.

Glossary

Arctic The cold regions around the North Pole.

Cannibalism When an animal eats another animal of the same species for food.

Carnivorous An animal that eats the flesh of other animals for food.

Climate The weather conditions in a particular place measured over a long period of time.

Depression A sunken or hollow place on an object.

Extinct When there are no living members of a particular species.

Gallbladder A small pouch found in some species of animals, including humans, that stores the bile produced by the liver.

Genetic Relating to the genes, which pass on characteristics from one generation of a species of living organism to the next.

Inhospitable A place that is difficult to live in because of its harsh conditions.

Kelp Types of large, brown seaweed that grow in "underwater forests" in shallow oceans.

Litter A group of several young animals born to a mother at one time.

Nutritious Food that is highly efficient in providing the body with the things it requires to be healthy.

Satellite A manmade object that orbits the planet from space. Satellites can be used to transmit signals and monitor particular objects or living organisms on Earth.

Sedate To put an animal to sleep for a period by giving them a drug.

Talisman An object that is thought to bring good luck or have magical powers.

Index